GARY SOTO

Junior College

GARY SOTO

Junior College

CHRONICLE BOOKS
SAN FRANCISCO

Acknowledgements

Most of the poems have appeared in the following magazines: *The Bellingham Review,
Boston Review, Crazy Horse, Denver Quarterly, Green Mountains Review, Harper's, Hayden's
Ferry Review, the Iowa Review, Massachusetts Review, Michigan Quarterly, New England
Review, Ontario Review, Poetry, Prairie Schooner, The Threepenny Review, TriQuarterly,* and
Witness.

"Some History," "The History of Science," "The Skeptics," "Getting Ahead," and
"Pagan Life" first appeared in *Poetry.*

Library of Congress Cataloging-in-Publication Data:
    Soto, Gary.
        Junior College : poems / Gary Soto.
        96 p.   15.2 x 22.8 cm.
        ISBN 0-8118-1543-9
        1. Junior College students – United States – Poetry. 2. Children's—
        United States—Poetry. I. Title.
        PS3569.072J86 1977
        811.54—dc20   96-36049
                                                                                CIP

Printed in the United States.

Book and cover design: Michael Osborne Design
Cover illustration copyright © 1997 by José Ortega

Distributed in Canada by
Raincoast Books
8680 Cambie Street
Vancouver, B.C. V6P 6M9

10 9 8 7 6 5 4 3 2

Chronicle Books
85 Second Street
San Francisco, CA 94105

www.chroniclebooks.com

THIS BOOK IS FOR SANDOR WEINER

CONTENTS

ONE

TWO

ONE

INFERIOR DOG

By third grade, by the time I was peeking
Beneath my scabs and the meat of hurt
And shame, I was pulling myself
Into trees and studying my dog,
Whom I loved but knew to be inferior,
Not like David's shiny beagle,
Not like Lassie who barked at us,
His audience of inferior people.
"Brownie," I called from my branch,
And my dog just shivered on the porch,
Whipped by the shadows of an oleander.
My dog was born tired.
When I took him on walks,
His head noosed in clothesline rope,
He climbed the street, panting
As he passed through each snotty taunt,
Purplish tongue dripping
Saliva that broke like mercury.
My heart broke, too,
When I saw the better dogs shake paws
And roll their happiness on the grass
And, in the spring air,
Plunge their happiness into frisky female dogs.
I looked at my dog and looked at myself —
One fight left his ear
Between a stray dog's teeth,
And left me in a circle of shame.
Later, oh my God,
I shoved my dog like a bully
And shook him through my hot tears
Because he could only walk and pant
And lick the bottoms of his front paws.
He was born tired, perhaps at the end
Of a day when workers, all creased,
All shiny and wet in every living hole,

Were holstering their angry hammers.
And I was born with shame
Because I helped my dog into the back seat
Of our car. I let him lay curled,
His better eye looking at the headliner,
Calm for this short drive,
Where at the end he would not walk or pant,
Or upon hearing his scolded name, Brownie!
Raise his tired head. Through milky eyes,
Through fistful of pulled fur,
He would not groan – What now, boy?

WHAT ARE YOU SPEAKING?

A friend said it was OK to be someone else,
That you didn't always have
To be Mexican. So,
During Lent I wanted to be Italian,
A change that would bring me closer to the Pope.
The next day I listened
To my friend Little John, then his mother,
A woman from the old country.
His mother said, "Whatsa madda?"
I heard this when Little John peeled skin
From his finger, when he meant to peel potato.
Little John bowed his head and started crying,
A spark of blood leaping behind his fingers.
Again she asked, this time louder: "Whatsa madda?"
He then really cried,
And I left my job
Of peeling shrimp and ran out of the house.
I thought she would start hitting him
For crying, and that maybe his mother
Would look at me and think I needed some too.
I walked down the street, and repeated,
"What is the matter? What's a matter?
Whats madder. Madda! Whatsa madda
Madda." I stomped out these words
On a cement as hard as the front of my head.
I sucked in the spring air, dizzy with blossoms.
I could feel that I was someone else,
And that maybe I could stay this
Way for a week, then go back to who I was.
When a boy on a tricycle ran over
My shoes, I shot, "Whatsa madda, madda!"
For two blocks I thought
I was speaking Italian,
And that if the Pope, by miracle, showed up
On our street he would recognize me

As one of his own. He would ask,
"Whatsa madda, Gary?" I would suck
In the plugs of my dirty nose,
And answer, "Madda? Little John's
A madda." Since the Pope probably knew a lot,
He would know madda was happening
At Little John's house
And some at mine.
The Pope would pat my head
And put me on his bouncing knee
For a long story, Biblical and dangerous,
Baby Jesus between two dry humps
Of a camel, and fleeing two thousand years
From madda.

BUDDHA, CHRIST & THE CLOCK

I knew Buddha with his belly laugh,
And Christ with his ribs
Deep with the shadows of an ancient grief.
I knew clocks, too, the twist of the knob —
Slashing long hand and small hand hobbling to keep up.
All three sat on my brother's desk
And made me worry about my own dying.
With watery clouds living behind my eyes,
I crossed myself and prayed in bed,
My hands folded under my head, both feet skyward.
Eyes closed, I prayed
With most of my heart until I saw Buddha and Christ
Sitting together on an ancient rock.
Neither of them was arguing. Buddha was pulling
On an earlobe, fat as a pear on a tree,
And Christ was touching one of his wounds,
Gapes like the mouths of pulsating fish.
It was dusk. The stream was hauling
The sunlight west, where Rome lay in incense
And scandal. I wanted to ask
About my sick lungs, vest of yellowish ooze,
And wanted to ask about my three sins —
Rock, flesh, and toad run over by my bike.
I was nine. I had pared skin from my thumb
And was worried about disease.
I got up from bed, wobbling, my heart bled of most
Of its sorrow. I looked closely at these gods
On my brother's desk, and then the clock,
Its hands cutting wedges in its round face.
I weighed Buddha and Christ in my palms,
Surprised that they were light, not like sin itself
Or the furrow one wears when the casket closes
And the sobbing starts. I picked up the clock,
Heavy with machinery, its oily gears and chimes.
I shook it once, hard,

And then laid it face down.
I knew the clock didn't care like Buddha or Christ,
And that my good thoughts mattered little.
It didn't ask for prayers.
When I stood the clock between these gods,
The cogwheel nevertheless nudged ahead
The iron-colored hours.

LISTENING TO JETS

My uncle liked the bluish rings from fighter jets
And liked the roar, something like water
Of his wife — my aunt — in the bathroom,
All faucets running hot. I was six, maybe seven,
And six or seven jets were lighting up our eyes.
They were scaring the black rags
Of birds pecking at the asphalt.
I was pecking at my palm, at the blister
From swinging a big-boy bat,
The collar of my T-shirt yanked like a noose.
We listened to this roar,
And followed the jets on the runway,
The purplish lights the most mysterious color
That ever splattered my eyes. This was 1961, dusk.
The heat had played with threads of our frayed anger.
Uncle had just beaten my aunt.
He would later take his beating in the driveway,
My other uncles fiery as those jets.
He knew this.
He parked at the airstrip to get his strength
From the purplish rings and the roar,
All faucets running on this summer day
When everything would come clean.

REINCARNATION

If you loved your cat, you'll become a cat.
If you loved your books, you'll become a book,
If you loved soup, you'll become soup.
This is an Eastern religion.

(True, I've hugged my cats and books,
And rowed many a large spoon through Sunday *menudo*.)

If you loved your wife, you'll become that wife.
You can't become yourself, whom you hate
In mirrors or the convex shine of prison ladles.
But if you loved yourself,
Then would you return as you were,
So likable in your Christmas tie and retirement ring?

Religion kills me.
My altar is stacked beer cans,
The cigarette an incense
Of ungodly times.
For my reincarnation, I climb out of bed
With my old lady and book, with my cat in the corner,
His arched back mad with the electricity of lice.
I want my coffee to pleat my mouth when I sip.
Now bring on a bowl of *menudo*,
My ancestral soup, my Sunday-morning cure,
This slaughter of *tripas*
Still full of fight when my jaws clamp
And I choke them all down.

GUILT AND THE IRON LUNG

Guilt was a good way
Of getting things done, like when
Mom said, "You don't love me."
I stuck my hands into the dishwater,
The suds pink from something like meat
Or shame, which was like guilt,
Like that color that passed
Over a face. Guilt forced me to open
The face of my sandwich, pink with meat,
Bloody with tomato slaughtered by a knife.
I knew that the poor of the world
Were not eating. I worried about this,
And worried when I rattled my can door-to-door
For the cause of polio and the boy
In the iron lung. It was spring,
And instead of playing baseball,
I collected money for children
Who could only bat their eyelashes.
Mother said they had to stay in the iron lung,
And now and then friends would come by
And ask, How are you doing, champ?
I was worried for them and, I guess, myself.
I pushed my hands into my own pockets —
The stern faces of dead presidents
Rolled into my own can,
A jamboree of coins.

                    I was scared
Of the iron lung — a summer of
Swimming in ditches,
Where bacteria was a yellowish lather
And frogs leaped sideways and didn't care
If we hit them with rocks. On porches,
I rattled my can and asked people
To help — a crutch of bad news

For the southern twins in Arkansas,
And some happening here,
A boy with a leg wilted like celery,
The other getting worse.
They fiddled in their pockets
And the pockets of their sunny aprons.
I rattled my can like a beggar
And remembered the ditches running high as a fever
And the poor frogs huddled together,
Their legs fractured by disease
And our hurled rocks.

HAND WASHING

I would wash my hands
After opening the refrigerator,
After looking at the lunchmeat and tomatoes,
The blimp-shaped pickles in cloudy water.
I would take out this food,
Then wash my hands before I flopped
Baloney on whole wheat, and then wash them again
Before I pulled up a chair,
Using my knuckle only. I wrapped
My sandwich in a paper napkin and ate facing
The wall lit with sunlight against feathery shadows.

I nearly gave up going to Mass —
Chalice that was a smudge of tubercular disease
And incense that fortified pneumonia.
I knew the priests were really good people
But knew they shook hands with the dying,
I was worried about moisture nestled on the hairs
Of their knuckles. I considered this matter
And considered their robes as they swished
Across the altar. I knew they often coughed
Into their hands,
Then said, "forgive us our sins. . . ."
After Mass, I used my shoulder
To get into the washroom, then scald my hands
With really hot water, then climb upstairs
To eat a donut. I didn't shake
Anyone's hand, just nodded and made my eyes
Kind of wide, my pupils filling
With friendly light. I talked using
Only a little bit of my mouth — no telling
If where you were standing a person
Had coughed and left disease floating in the air.

I knew Catholics were coming around
To talk in tongues
And I knew that weeping men
Were coming out of really large closets —
Sex was that lily you wagged
Over the grave of innocent people.
I rattled my newspaper and read about them,
The new Catholics who held hands in prayer.
For a while, when my hair was black,
I attended the young adult group
And despised the air when we had to hold hands.
One week I noticed
Three out of sixteen were coughing,
And a week later seven of the sixteen.
I was never good at math but knew eight was next,
And was beginning to feel a rock-like scrape
Inside my throat. I stopped going
And instead read the Bible by the window
And considered the fly, dead on the sill,
And the plagues marching through Egypt
Toward hometown Fresno.

I liked my wife to wash her hands
And asked her often not to touch her teeth
In public places. She went along
And started pushing open doors
Using only her shoulder.
I taught her how to pull a chair away
From the table and to seal an envelope
Without touching the flap.
She listened with her washed hand
Covering mine. She was nice to me,
And said nothing
When she saw me washing not only
My hands but wrists and elbows,

Knobby points that touched public places
And maybe the edges of our dinner plates,
An accident that could cause disease.
If she had asked, What are you doing?
I would have looked up from the basin,
Curl of steam like incense,
And answered, I'm saving myself, and you too, love.

THE ACTORS

On television some actors played people
Who were dead, like cowboys
Or Romans spanking a savage lather
From their chariots.
A whole cavalry fell from cliffs,
Arrows in their backs.
A sailor got his leg hooked on ropes
And was sucked into the sea.
Indians didn't have much
Of a chance, even with smears of warpaint.
I wondered how they felt, the actors I mean,
Playing dead people. How could they
Feign the sickness of a poisoned emperor,
Sigh the last sigh, drop a glass from limp fingers,
Then answer to the director's "Cut!"

On Dr. Kildare,
A boy had swallowed a toy harmonica.
The good doctor picked up a clipboard
And said, "We need to operate."
I breathed in and out, my lungs like a harmonica.
I was nine, maybe younger.
I felt the noise in my lungs.
My brother swung his body on the couch
And told me a nurse tested his hearing at school.
With earphones on his head, he had to raise
His left hand, then his right,
Then both flew up when he felt the injections,
Like porcupines, in both ears.
He told me this after watching Dr. Kildare.
I wiggled a worm of washed finger into my ear,
Poked, then raised both hands like spears.
That night, I lay in bed,
Scared. I made out the sounds
Of the house, the creak and snap of wood.

I marched the actors behind my closed eyes —
Dr. Kildare with a butterknife in one hand.
I made him put the blade
Into his own ear, poke, then say to me,
"See, it doesn't hurt." I breathed in and out,
My own harmonica of disease inside me,
And tried to get into practice —
Child athlete with a body of straw,
Cough and wheeze, the flutter of eyes,
Head drooping, dead in his third-grade role.

EVOLVED PEOPLE

At 7-Eleven, my half-brothers ate two hotdogs,
Stuffed them down quickly, then bought
A soda, no ice, just a liquid
To slosh in their bellies from noon
'til six. The cashier asked,
Anything else? My brothers,
With hot dogs in their throats,
Shook their heads and croaked, No, dude.
Outside, they laughed and they may have patted
Their bellies, the buddhas of Me First
And You Later. They retold this story
While barbecuing chicken and hamburgers,
This meal lifted from the local Safeway.
Smoke from the coals stung my eyes.
I told them they shouldn't steal,
And they told me to shut up.
Jimmy told me everyone steals.
He said, Looka my finger.
I looked at it, pink as a fat sausage.
He asked me, You see a ring there?
I told him no. He said, That's the point, bro.
It got stole. He then turned the patties
And fiddled with the chicken wings,
Crippled skin hissing over the coals.
He took a swig of beer with one eye on me,
And said, I know what you are, Gary.
You ain't nothing but a evolved people.
I sipped my soda, piled high with ice,
And said, Nah, man, I ain't evolved.
I'm your brother. Jimmy crushed his beer can
And hopped our low fence into the neighbor's yard.
He plucked two ripe tomatoes
And shouted, How about cucumbers?
I nodded my head, scared that the neighbor
Would come out on his back porch. But Jimmy grunted

Over the fence and sliced the tomatoes,
The seed spilling like teeth.
He could see that I didn't like what he had done,
And he laughed, You got a wino belt on.
I looked down at my belt, stylishly cowboy.
He asked, How come you dress like a sissy?
And then shoved a black hotdog onto my plate.
For two weeks, I feared for my brothers.
I thought they would get caught at the 7-Eleven,
Both of them handcuffed and swallowing the last
Of their free hotdogs.

When I was invited
To a party for an Australian
Poet wearing ironed jeans,
I listened to a pencil-neck scholar
Say things like this: Swedenborgian traditions
Are contained by the objective foundations
That began in Blake's time.
This very strange talk
Made me think I had stared directly at
A bare lightbulb — a galaxy of blinding spots
That signaled real learning.
Some guests listened,
But others just nodded their heads
As they felt for the little meats on toothpicks.
Their wine glasses sloshed Chardonnay
And bathed the good cells
Inside the many folds of brain matter.
I didn't drink that afternoon.
I nibbled melon balls
And looked out the window —
The spots in front of my eyes were gone.
In the street,
Two boys bending a car antenna.

When I knocked on the window, the boys laughed
And whacked a bike chain against a tree.

When I turned to join the others,
I thought I saw my brother by the food table,
Brother stabbing the pinkie-sized sausages,
Letting them roll into his mouth,
Greedily. But it was a Teutonic guest,
Arms like clubs. He ate, head bowed,
And for all I know, he was the owner
Of the car with a bent antenna.
He could have been my brother or stepfather,
Or a friend of the family shoving
Chicken parts onto a grill, in summer.
I put down my plate of melon balls.
180 miles from home,
I was somewhere between evolved
And unevolved. The guest looked at me,
Eyes like a snow-blind beast. The tomato bled
From the torturous end of his sparkling fork.

PHONE CALLS

It'll hurt, the voice said on the telephone,
And that was enough for me to hang up
And stare at the slash of sunlight
On the wall. The hangers began to bang
In the closet. The dead flies
On the windowsill spun slightly
When I opened the door and studied the car
Across the street, a sparrow possibly locked
In its grill. I closed the door again
And answered the phone in the hallway.
The voice again said, It'll hurt.
I hung up. I walked through two rooms
And stood in the kitchen. The faucet dripped
Over the chicken breasts my wife left
To defrost. I tapped the breast with a knuckle,
As I might my heart, and looked out
The front window. The car was gone.
A dog heaved a milky glob in my driveway
And rain ticked in the throats
Of our wooden gutters.
I listened to the blue thump
Of my pulse. I counted to ten,
Then let it go. I looked at the telephone,
Cradle of black misery, then returned
To the kitchen. I glanced out
The window. A neighbor played harmonica
On his front steps. Didn't he know
It was going to hurt, and the hurt
Was what we lived for, bewildered and nervous.
Even in sleep,
Our eyes searched behind their lids.

THE TUBA PLAYER

We knew volcanic pimples
And boredom, that panting dog
Chained under the orange
Tree. We knew two dirty jokes
And a tickling joy —
Sand poured through the hour
Glass of puny hands.
We knew boatloads
Of desire. We woke
To heat-struck nose bleeds
From hot sleeping,
Our dolphins flogged
Under an anchor print
Of bedsheets. Let me
Admit it: Annette Funicello
Perked up the interest
Of even blind boys,
And on our street
The quick peek of bald pussy
Was one grimy quarter
And three licks
From a popsicle.
Gourmet was a foreign country,
We thought, and Mexico
Started at the borders
Of your own yard
With hubcaps cemented
In our iron grille fence —
A nice touch for loud people.
Winos were old clothes
Come alive, and, my god,
Some mother's precious daughter
At the turn of
The century cried
In a greasy ballroom gown.

I stopped my bike
And wished her faith.
She was drunk, I remember,
Legs splayed in front
Of Let Me Out bail bonds
And her crying
So deep, the earth
Was already inside her.
As I say, we knew suffering.
Lice arrived in our
Hair in winter
And left by late spring,
Along with migratory birds.
And that spring
Of 1968, before the heat
Settled more fights,
Our one Mexican tuba player
In the marching band
Threw himself from
A billboard. Amigo,
My dear reader with a cup of coffee,
He wasn't whistling Dixie
Through his front teeth
When he hit.

YOU'VE GONE TOO FAR

My youngest brother fiddled a tie on his neck,
That satchel of pinkish skin and bad-ass threats.
He pushed an elephant leg into his slacks.
He shrugged into a jacket.
He slapped his face with the angry sting of Brut
And jingled coins in his pockets,
A jamboree of quarters and hot dimes.
This was the year he dealt stocks and mutual funds.
All day, he put a phone to his mouth and chimed,
China Fund is growing and India is crushing
The shit out of – excuse me – superceding
The European Market. I was happy for him.
He had evolved, and so had my uncle Shorty,
Now a foreman on his crew.
He had left his common-law wife
For her daughter – shame that didn't redden his face,
Even after he became a Jehovah's Witness,
Trumpeting the Good News. My cousins
Were no longer Mexican rednecks,
Those "He-He-He Sonbitches" you pulled up to
At a red light, their eyes flecked with drugs.
They tended their families,
Held down jobs. My toughest brother was swatting
The holy hell out of flames in the foothills,
And winning. He was a firefighter,
His hair the curl of black smoke.

Now taxpayers, we stopped jamming parking meters
For free time,
And punching weak-eyed biology teachers.
Still, one brother didn't like the way I dressed.
At Christmas, he tied me up on the front lawn
And growled, You're a pussy.
We wrestled and then sat on the grass,
Arguing about the levels of pussiness.

He told me, seriously, that I had evolved too far,
And then returned inside to the canned ham
With its single crown
Of pineapple. Family huddled against me
Near the Christmas tree, heavy with
Lights and the Ho-Ho of a brown-face Santa
Snagged at the swap meet.

My family feared that I had evolved too far.
They tore my book in half,
And stripped me of my Italian belt.
This was Christmas and this was fun.
We were drunk, all seven of us,
Just as Andy Williams began to sing on television.
Four brothers got in the car and drove to a 7-Eleven,
And there, with the strings of ham between
Our teeth, little brother yelled at the clerk,
What are you lookin' at, you rag-head asshole?
Then he pushed me into a rack
Of Hostess Sno-balls. We crushed them,
And then bought them. In the parking lot,
I explained that Benjamin Franklin liked to drink –
Ben said our elbows
Bent neatly taking our cups to our mouths.
Jimmy told me to shut up. We drove in circles,
And when I began to yak sno-balls and beer,
My brothers squeezed my shoulders, almost tenderly,
Squeezed them and said, That's better, dude,
We're glad you're back.

WHICH GOD DO YOU BELIEVE?

By 10th grade I believed
The God of You're-Not-Going-To-Get-What-You-Want.
I spent my time preaching this gospel
To my right hand,
The same one that wanted to run its oils
Over at least three pear-shaped rumps.
I bit the bitterness of my fingernails,
And spit my parings at this God,
Then played my zipper up and down on my jacket.
It was something to do,
The teeth meeting and parting,
Its sound a metallic, gnat-like whine.
Maybe from some starry distance
We were all gnats, whining with combs in our hair
Or smoothing out our crushed Valentines,
Maybe pounding our fists on steering wheels
And driving over country toads that got in the way.
We whined our loneliness, then crept
Into bed with a hard stick in our oily hands.

So? So suffering in both legs,
I walked the rickets of adolescence
And held onto Scott, crutch of brotherly love.
I believed in my God and hydrotherapy.
We bathed in a pubic – I mean public – fountain,
Our legs shimmering like tunas beneath the surface
Of the water. The summers were hot
Behind each metal snap or cracked button,
Hot where our wet footprints were an oasis for ants.
I asked, God of You're-Not-Going-To-Get-What-You-Want,
Would you allow me to bump into a breast
Between second and third period?
May I peek at some white panties
And swig sorrow from an icy cold Pepsi?
I asked with water in my hair, in my ears,

In the cyclops of my overgrown belly button.
No, this God of mine yelled,
And, Shit no, don't you even try to dance!

On this late June night,
23 years later,
My hometown is a pulsating clam of desire.
I can't eat at this plate. Two gnats
Are arguing over the hair in my ears.
My fingernails are pared to bloody moons.
Here is Scott, brother in a lounge chair,
And here is hippie Dave in his tie-dyed T-shirt.
Here the girls I liked on a back yard lawn —
Hilda, Corina, and you too, La Baby.
I look skyward. God is watching
With a melon rind in his hand.
I whine. I take my plate and iceless drink
And I sit with Hilda, hatchets of mascara
Over each eye. I ask, Hilda,
Which God do you believe?
She swallows and says, What?
I tell her that there is either God of Life
Or God of Nothing. She shows me
Her front two teeth. She gets up,
Her bottom waddling like a flock of geese.
I have no hope in my lounge chair,
No beauty to lower my face toward.
God throws his rind on the lawn. Therefore,
I am a beast tearing into the grilled legs
Of a helpless chicken.

SMALL TALK AND CHECKERS

I slip into my old robe.
I weave my beard into a noose.
I set a checkerboard on a trash can—
Three flies for me and my out-of-work friend.
I call him Smiley. "Smiley," I say,
"It's your move." He chuckles
And raises his peppered hand to his throat,
That satchel of loose skin. Smiley scratches
His nose and shoves a checker.
He says, "Is that corn
Or your teeth?" I ignore him
And leap like crazy over the board.
I rub my hands together,
Friction that was desire ten years before.
The flies settle at the edge
Of boredom and filth,
Their fuzzy bottoms hugging the board.

The sun presses westward.
A boy on a bike tosses the newspaper,
The news sorted equally between the dead
And the living. The wind stirs
The flies on our throats. When a girl taunts,
"Hey, old man!" Smiley and I both look up,
Feeble men eager at our final call.

PROFILE IN RAIN

Having polished my shoes,
Having rolled my laces with a little spit,
I put a matchbook in the bottom of my left shoe
And looked at myself in the mirror:
The mirror was right. My teeth were huge
For my 14-year-old head.
Still, I left the house and circled my loneliness
With two other strays, their backs wet,
Their fangs worn down to meager pebbles.
I circled my hometown. A girl was somewhere,
Perhaps behind that kitchen window:
A bored lass writing her name in the crumbs
Gathered at the warmth of a chrome toaster.
A vamp was combing her hair
And rereading her boyfriend's sloppy letter.
A towhead tomboy was fussing in her closet —
A skirt with chains and the heavy hearts of anchors.
I looked down at my dog friends. Rain clinged
To their faces. When I spoke, my breath was white.
When I put a finger to a steamy car window,
I wrote, "God, help me."
I returned home to look at myself in the mirror:
My teeth were even bigger,
Now that my hair was matted to my head.
I took off shoes
And socks. I pulled out the soggy matchbook —
The choir of matches and the shifty words
Of a correspondence school:
"Draw this profile. You may have talent."
I considered the girl with half a face,
Sweetheart with not much to go on.
Rain fell from my hair when I picked up a pen
And, biting my bottom lip, started with her eyes.

BODILY RESPONSES TO HIGH MASS

I put on a white shirt and tie,
And let my body weep sweat
In the third pew from the front,
Let it stand with my weight
On my left leg, then my right.
I bowed my head. The homily
Had nothing to do with me —
Jesus walking on water
And scaring the hell out of fishermen.
I yawned. Tears plunged from my eyes,
The ancient salts sliding in
The grooves of my Catholic school years.
I scratched. I traced the lines
In my palms, those pinkish rivers,
And noticed my hand created a wind
In the name of the Father, Son, and Holy Spirit.
My untested loins twitched when I genuflected,
And my chest rose and fell like empires.
The church was stuffy. I wept sweat
Until I was a jungle of pagan smells.
By then, Jesus was done walking on water.
By then, Mass was half over.
My knees hurt. The buttons on
My shirt had yellowed. When I arrived,
I had been clean shaven, and now a beard
Glistened in my lap. But there was more,
More because sin was a matter of heads
Or tails. The priest set Jesus back on the water.
Alright, I thought, I get the point.
I will be good. The lion will lay down
With the lamb, and all that.
My youth passed. I shrunk like a mushroom,
And blue veins appeared on my arm.
Mass ended. I was an old man shuffling down
The aisle, pausing every third pew.

I smacked my lips as I headed outside.
I descended spiral steps into the basement –
White powdery donuts, those stacked halos,
Were my heavenly reward.

SUSPICIONS

I suspected some nuns raked
Their palms over their shaved heads,
A bristly feeling that tickled their skin,
Or on rainy nights unwrapped butcher paper
Where shorn hair lay like a whip.
I suspected some wanted to hit us really hard
And others wanted to peer out
The classroom window,
Oblivious to our crippled fractions,
Poor spelling, the crayoned Christ with five holes.
I suspected that if I could get through 3rd grade
I would make mother happy,
Mother with all her hair, her lipstick,
Her sleeve gray from her work of peeling potatoes.
I suspected I was not right in the head
And wanted only to sit in the same chair,
Hands on the table, a pen in the right pocket
And a short pencil in my left.
I didn't want to cause problems,
Like the boy who wrote "fuck" on his arm,
Or the girl who peed serenely in class.
I wanted to see the blackboard.
I wanted to write
In my own jittery script, The Lord is with me,
Then fold this piece of paper
And wear it close to my rabbit-thump of a heart.
I didn't talk much back then.
I suspected that I was good
Because I felt light and most of my thoughts
Were on the dead, like my father,
A four-prong twig in the ground.
Some of my thoughts were on Africa,
A thorny place
If you had to run from lions and pagans,
And some of my thoughts were on my guardian angel,

An invisible but holy shadow
That brought on barking dogs.
I walked slow for my angel to keep up,
And once muttered, "I'm here. It is me."
We were at Mass for a run-over student,
A fresh pair of eyeglasses on his studious face.
I prayed for this boy with weight on my knees
And none on my shoulders. Lightning cracked,
Rain poured like sorrow,
And my lungs reaped
The dead boy's portion of air.

THE CHARITY OF LA SEÑORA LARA

Once I worked
For a nearly deaf *vieja,*
And she worked to get in my way,
Her grin chattering over my shoulders.
I raked an already raked yard,
Gathered dropped plums into a bag, swept
And hoed the life out of a flowerbed.
I roofed the doghouse with flattened tuna cans
And beat the mites from a rug.
Later, on the lawn, we stood together
And stared at a wobbly sprinkler throwing out cool seed
Of water. I worked two hours,
Screamed in her good ear for my pay,
And then walked home,
Musing over the value of unearned money.

She was more than *loca*
When I returned, weeks later, and she asked
From the porch, "*¿Quién es?* Who are you?"
Plastic fruit clacked in her straw hat
And the autumn wind rippled her print dress
And her furry slippers. She clicked her fingers,
"You're the barber's boy, no?"
I shook my head. I was neither the barber's boy
Nor the preacher's spoiled son.
I was neither Italian nor Jew,
Syrian nor Armenian. I was neither the lost lamb
Nor a stray child walking in the sandals of a gracious god.

I made a raking motion with my hands.
She giggled, remarked, "I am a woman,"
And scratched the one hair on her chin.
I gathered invisible oranges,
Shoveled a flower bed, spanked rugs on a clothesline,
And hammered boards for the rain shook from a cloud.

She shook her head, eyes clear as the zeros
Plugged through a road sign.

"You know, *señora*," I screamed, "I'm your working boy."
Her smile rattled the banana and cherries on her hat.
"*Mi'jo*," she wept into my shoulders, "welcome home!"

THE PEACH PIT

My friend said, "Man, I'd give anything to see
You sweat." Right then, in my mother-in-law's yard,
I put on one leather glove and started shoveling.
He ate a peach while watching me build a froth
Under my arms and a rain forest in my hair.
When he left, mightily impressed,
I put on the other glove
And slowed my pace. By then, a beard of gnats
Grew from my chin. By then,
A cricket of pain chirped in my spine.
I shoveled and
Whistled the poet's slave song, "Give Me Money."
I wiped my brow and stroked my beard
Of gnats. Since no one was looking,
I retired to a chair, gloves in my lap,
And admired the poetry of my work:
One hole for rose bush
Or perhaps poor carcass of a struck dog.
A sparrow jumped at the edge
Of the hole and flew away.
The neighbor's cat then sniffed,
A clear bead of boredom in each eye.

This was toward evening.
My mother-in-law padded out in furry slippers
And remarked, "It's not deep enough,"
A line I have lived with
Since I first sharpened a #2 pencil.
Still, with my shoe,
I prodded the peach pit into the hole,
Where sweet-toothed ants could lick
Their antennas and get to work.
I packed the earth. I shook a garden hose
Over this plot, the dirt now black
As my hair at birth. The cat returned,

Followed by the sparrow.
My mother-in-law shrugged
And said, "It's better from seedlings, not seeds."
With both gloves off and
Rings of blisters on my palms, what was I
But a prophet working his hard-headed faith.

TWO

THE HISTORY OF SCIENCE

Nicholas Fedorovich Fedorov believed in science,
Believed you could die and let out a thirsty yawn
In your grave. After all, the duty of science
Was to revive you decades later,
You the refreshed man in need of a shave
And new set of continental clothes.
He dreamed such thoughts in 1859,
A Russian winter with black birds
Eating black ice. If you stepped off the curb,
A ragman's cart could crush your foot.
The foot could become infected,
Grow large as a bass. This occurred
To Mr. Fedorov, I read,
And he smoked his puny cigarettes
And sipped brandy, not in the least scared.
Science would bring him back
If he died with one foot larger than the other.
He would lie in his grave,
Thumbs touching and his watch stopped at 12:34.
Decades would pass, and birds, too.
By then, by the time science bubbled over test tubes
And the like, by the time Jesus was revived,
More scared the second time around,
Mr. Fedorov would lift himself from his casket,
Eyes blinded by this thing, that wonder,
Our luminescence of question marks. . . the lightbulb.

Mr. Fedorov, Russian dreamer with ice on your beard,
You have not seen the emergency room in Oakland.
They are calling #14.
My own ticket is #56. I stepped on a tack,
And my foot may grow stinky as a trout.
They call #15, a boy with a bandage over one eye.
They call #16 and #17, twins with bad colds.
They call #18, but he can't get up, old man spider.

They skip him and shout for #19,
Immigrant mother with babies in her arms
And another in her belly. All I need
Is an injection, some prayers.
I read greasy magazines
And wait thinking of you, Mr. Fedorov,
Still yawning in your grave,
Blind to the invention of lightbulbs
And the new disease that crawls up your arms.
You have not seen Oakland at night,
The screams and coughing and palpitating hearts.
You're in your grave, thin as twigs,
And you missed some of the best wars
And the best stories of war. Famines blew
Like sand in Africa and Jews stood on rattling trains.
In Chile, the president sneezed
And the whole country waved a Kleenex for the man.
Comrade Fedorov, your watch stopped at 12:34,
Not a minute too soon.

SOME HISTORY

Sumerians carried really long swords,
And Aztecs handled clubs with glassy rocks
Serrating the tips. Pygmies hid
In the savage grass
With blow darts as tall as they.
Bad-ass Genghis Khan had no second thoughts
About fitting your head onto a stick —
You the missionary,
Now the bloody head looking westward,
Lids half-closed and in view of the praying Pope,
His thoughts something like, "Mama mia!"
I swallowed some of this history
And turned the page. Incas threw
Really good-looking nymphs from temples,
And the gentle Chinese poet with incense curling
Around his beard was dangerous — bamboo worked
Under your fingernails
While he talked about the long life
Of oxen. I knew Germans stomped through Europe
And the Japanese could push a bayonet
In the left breast
Of the woman tattooed on your back.
(You the corporal from Missouri caught by surprise,
Your tin can of spook-eyed sardines
Spilling into the Asian earth.)
Where is it safe? I thought. The Eskimos
Harpooned huge whales,
And the Moors brought down swords on the necks
Of stubborn camels. The French priests
Skipped over rivers of blood,
And in Nagasaki
The shadows of children were blown onto walls.
This scared me, too — disease in pitted molars.
I turned the page and began to worry.
My best friend was a boy in an iron lung

And two girls in leg braces
Devouring pamphlets about presidents
We never heard about. My arms failed to respond
To push-ups. I coughed a lot at night.
I knew God let people die when it was
The best thing to do. I knew
The river people
Flowed west on the Tigris
And that little beauty existed in our yard,
Not even in the apple tree, where blossoms
Were torn by the greedy hunger of bees.

NOTES FOR SOCIOLOGY

These boys own the sun-bleached grass,
Spiked with bees and mosquitoes.

These old men own a stride of sand
Where horseshoes are tossed.
They stand with hands on hips,
Faces pleated, heads square as loaves of bread.
These are working men with sand at their feet.

I'm in the bleachers blistered from the heat,
Thinking of a shoe I stupidly lost
In a wave at Pismo Beach.
(The moon had gone crazy the night before,
And when we woke, the waves were huge,
White-tipped like teeth.
My shoe floated off without my foot
And was sucked down like all we'll ever know.)
I peel green paint from the bench,
Grit under my fingernails. I watch the skirts
Of the eucalyptus rattle in wind
And chrome wink from the fender of a passing car.
I watch a dog hurry across the lawn,
Something like a shoe in its mouth.
It hurries away, and we can't keep up.

Grass or sand or even sea.
The playing slows as the body thickens.
Lead pits our teeth, dirt clots our hearing.
We spit into white handkerchiefs.
A horseshoe is tossed,
Not unlike our bones. But when we come down,
We come down on the iron spike.

THE SKEPTICS

Pyrrho of Elis and Sextus Empiricus were Skeptics,
Two big-shot thinkers who argued
Over figs, wine, and the loveliness of their sex.
I crowed to my brother about them,
And one evening,
With Fig Newton crumbs in our mouths,
I was Pyrrho and Rick was Sextus,
Both of us skeptical about getting good jobs.
I said, "Brother Sextus,
What will you render on the canvas
When you're all grown up?" He chewed
On his Fig Newton and answered, "Pyrrho,
My young flame, I will draw the reality
Of dead dogs with their feet in the air."
I crowed, "Wow, Rick — I mean Sextus — that's awesome!"
In sandals, we went down to the liquor store,
Each of us in our imaginary Greek robes,
And stole a quart of beer. Neither of us
Was a skeptic when we swigged on that quart
And walked past the house
Where a woman hammered on walnuts,
The rise and fall of her buttery hand quivering
The two hairs on my chest. We had figs and wine,
And what we Skeptics needed
Was three strokes of that hammering.
I flowed over in my robe
And said, "We're Brother Skeptics,
Ruled by cautious truths." She smiled,
Hammer raised, and said, "Sure you are."
Right away we got along, a womanly skeptic
With a nice swing. I sat on the steps,
A young man with his figs, his wine,
And, with my Greek name shed,
Reverent believer in a woman with hammer in hand.

EVERYTHING TWICE

Biology was a set of marble-colored tables
And gas spouts where we bloated up frogs.
Science scared me. But I knew
I had a chance if I bought the book
Early and read it with my lips moving,
Maybe twice, maybe with my roommate half-listening.
I tried chemistry. I tried astronomy,
Which was more like honest-to-goodness math
Than the star of Bethlehem shining down good news.
I was never good
At science. So at the beginning of spring
I leaned the elbows of my boredom
On a piss-colored desk.
But when our biology prof stumbled
Into the classroom wiping his mouth,
When he moved a chair out of the way
And still bumped into it, I knew I had a chance.
He was drunk. His bow-tie was a twisted-up
Twig and a nest of hair grew
From each ear. I looked to the skeleton
In the corner and smiled. A breeze stirred
The bones, which clacked on strings and wire.
With the classroom splayed with sunlight
And hope, the students sighed.
A few pencils rolled to the floor –
An easy grade for all. The prof slurred,
"Man was never created equal."
He fumbled for the chalk at the blackboard.
When he turned to us, chalk dust clung to his face.
For a moment, I don't think he knew where he was.
He touched his bowtie. He stuck a finger
Into a hairy ear
And repeated, "Man was never created equal,"
Took a step and stumbled into chairs. Right then
I knew I didn't even have to buy the book.

He was already repeating himself. Right there,
I looked out the window and sucked in
The spring air. Trees wagged blossoms
And the like. One petal would sway,
Then another, sway after slight sway,
A repetition that was endless
And beautiful in the uniquely scientific world.

WHAT IS YOUR MAJOR?

One spring I thought that maybe archeology
Was better than mortuary studies,
That a person scanned the wreck of a pagan temple
And by intuition commanded, "This is where we dig."
I knew people died like minutes,
And that someone had to.tie shoelaces one last time
And fiddle with the collars before the coffins,
Soft as pin cushions, were closed.
I knew they were similar, the ancient dead
Washed by the rise and fall of the Nile,
And the recent dead, like Mrs. White's husband,
Poor man whose head fit through the rollers
Of industrial machinery. I knew
Mr. White would go nowhere, even if his coffin rotted
And rain washed over his face,
Now narrow as a hatchet.
He wouldn't get up and scare me,
And the temples wouldn't litter
My back with goose bumps.
I had outgrown ghost stories,
And at night I was not in the least scared
Of petting my own flesh,
Eventual fodder for the carnivorous earth.
I was nineteen, in junior college,
Piling up units so that I could help the dead.
I wanted to use my hands,
Either by shoveling for pharaohs by the Nile,
Or, in the college basement under a twenty-watt bulb,
Patting rouge on a poor fellow,
Cooing, "Come on, friend, let's make a good show."

WESTERN CIVILIZATION

If I could remember that Ptolemy's beard wagged
Over maps, and Gutenberg rolled up
His sleeves and set type by a yellowish candle,
If I could subtract the deaths of Spartans
And add the dark furor of Persians,
I would finally get out of that class.
I would remove myself from the view of a woman
Sharing the inside of her thighs,
A little flowery panty bringing me down
To a B, possibly worse. I liked
The class and for the first four weeks
I traced the Nile River in our textbook,
And thought of Assyrians in their chariots,
And the Jews badmouthing the Romans,
And the Romans drinking their version
Of highballs at sunset, blood red
And already ancient on the backs
Of exhausted slaves. By week five
We were on rock-dry Greece,
And in week seven,
The Vandals were picking their teeth
With the bones of small children.
The Pope fathered children
And spent hours on his knees, bored
And turning his weighty rings clock-wise
On his pudgy fingers.
In England, bacteria attacked the throats
Of dirty villagers
And the plague arrived,
Coal-red in the eyes of slick rats.
I didn't like these pages, or week eleven,
When the young woman began to wear
Short pants, her calves the color of pears.
Spring made me sneeze, and once she said,
Gesundheit, which then introduced us

To Germany and the Teutonic warriors,
And then quickly to the bagpipes of Scotland,
Where sheep stood cloud-like
In the green fields. I carried my textbook,
Black with heavy words, and I carried
The sight of this young woman's panties,
Etched on the backs of my eyeballs.
I chewed my number 2 pencil,
Fodder for my loneliness.

I bit the hills of my knuckles,
A salty desire just before lunch.
I took the final exam, and was brought down
From a B to a whimpering C,
Distracted by her unbuttoned blouse
And the crossed and uncrossed legs –
Cleopatra opening shop on the shores of
My own creamy Nile . . .

DEAR JOURNAL

I went to a junior college
Where Teacher of the Year tripped
And skidded on her knees,
An awful fall that had her genuflecting,
A briefcase in each hand. She blinked
Tears and continued to her car,
For there was money to make
And a husband to whip
With desire. The anthro teacher,
A guy who wore medieval armor on weekends,
Said that he had the power
To keep his arm straight
Under the pressure of
Any Negro tight end in our glorious nation.
We lined up, his three-unit students,
And bent his arm like a slot machine
Until he was exhausted and tears rode
His creased face. The speed-reading teacher
Spoke in a minty breath,
Said our eyeballs would skate over the page
If we first stared at the color lavender
And let our tear ducts flow like steam on windows.
He demonstrated. He stared at lavender construction
Paper and cried over an article
Of a wet tea-cup terrier.
We read this story and two girls, one boy,
Forced up tears, too. So this
Was junior college, so this was me
Walking my loneliness from one class to another.
Listen up: from the counseling office
– trailer with solid, recap tires –
I heard a student cry behind its walls.
I listened, shamelessly,
And scurried away,
Fearing that sadness was contagious.

Later, in the typing room, before a boulder-sized
Machine the color of an elephant,
I heard a woman scream, "the ribbons are old!"
She typed standing up, the weight of her body
On each strike, and her underarms soggy by
The time she finished a perfect page.
I enrolled in logic that spring.
I began to think this:
A huge onion was buried under the campus
And its fumes were making us cry.
Our track team wept, our cheerleaders,
Our debate team with the wrong topic.
We wept when our college paper
Was printed upside down,
And when the sprinklers came on in rain.
The gardener, thumbs hurting from thorns,
Sobbed like a clown,
And the parking lot attendant made a face
When you ran over the tips of his hand-me-down boots.
We were sad, and we were crying,
For now the world was ugly.
The onion made good and bad students cry,
Even the stray dogs who sniffed our yellowish lawns.
My shoulders forced up weeping, too,
When I saw the counseling trailer was gone,
Four skid marks on the sidewalk.
Where it had sat, muddy dents in the ground,
Each pooled with the shine of previous tears.

CAREER COUNSELING

The mortuary students, those vampires with cool fingers,
Would get good jobs, for the world was filled
With the dying – grandmothers needling
Their last doilies and workers with their scalps
Feeding into industrial rollers.
The criminology students gathered
Near the bike racks, their compound eyes
Behind sunglasses. They searched for trouble,
Their hands at their sides where, in three months,
Colt 45s would snuggle in oily holsters.
In college, I stayed away
From these future cops. In World Religions,
I considered the priesthood.
In geology, I considered lighting up the world,
The bang of two rocks.
I took speed reading,
The equivalent of 19 cups of coffee,
And enrolled in biology – Mendel crosswiring peas in pods.
The nursing students hurried with clipboards,
And one day I followed them,
Like a dog, like insomniatic patient.

In junior college, I painted numbers on curbs,
The houses themselves as cold as tombstones.
I worked on my knees, right above the busy traffic
Of straight-ahead, no-bullshit ants.
I went from house to house. At the level
Of each porch I could reason this –
There was work for both mortuary and criminology students,
And somewhere in between the nurses were involved –
Their stethoscopes counting down the heartbeats.
I painted curbs and kept to myself.
One day, my counselor asked, What do you want to be?
He asked this on
A day when student nurses eyed my crippled walk,

When a mortuary student asked if I could play dead
And let him count my teeth and broken bones.
The newly graduated cops were meaner
Than thugs. They scolded those
Who walked on our reseeded lawns,
Scolded those in wheelchairs and on crutches.
I should leave town, I told myself,
And would have given
Some of my teeth to travel to Ireland or Scotland,
Somewhere cool. Or like a ghost,
I would have lived inside a tree
And come out only when it was dark, thus safe,
Untouchable as smoke. But I left his office
And returned to the curbs. With both knees wet
And sunlight bright as scissors,
I lowered my eyes and thought of the divisions of labor —
Me with house numbers, the vocational students
With good jobs, and, in my shadow, ants
With our human plunder descending into creaturely holes.

PAGAN LIFE

In history of religion,
I read that three-foot pagans carried five-foot spears,
Worshiped trees and hundred-pound pumpkins,
And after week-long hunts returned to their village
To throw their women in the dirt
And get some under the sun.
I licked my fingers and turned the page,
Looking for pictures. I found none,
Only more words. The bell rang,
And I left the class, 5'8", with no spear, no woman,
No tree to stand under and chant, "O, blessed Tree."
I was nineteen. I dragged my loneliness like a dead cat
To the levee. The water rushed black.
The wind whipped the eucalyptus,
That giraffe of trees.
I bent my head over the water
And shook buddha shaped tears into that ancient current.
Tires floated by,
The dead carcass of a suitcase,
And overturned kitchen tables with spindly legs
Jutting above the surface. I cried for the fish,
And the fish's cousin, a one-eyed toad in the reeds.
Then I picked up a stick, me the pagan,
And chased a gopher into a hole.
I grew small and powerful.
As I walked, I became deliriously wild
From carrying my ten-foot spear.
My footprints left dents in the sandy ground,
Footprints that slowly shortened
Until they were only inches apart. By then,
Ants followed my march, beetles and termites,
And one armadillo, a lock-jawed disciple.
By the time I reached town,
I was trouble for married and unmarried women.
I was no bigger than a thumb,

And my spear, Jesus Christ, tottered in my arms
And stirred the populace from their houses —
Wondrous girls climbing onto each other's shoulders
For a glimpse of the thing that sanctified the air.

FREUD IS MY FRIEND

In college, Freud was a picture in our textbook,
Little spade of hair on his chin.
My friend Ricky, now with a beard,
Bragged he went down
On his girlfriend at the drive-in movies.
How was it? I asked, and he said,
It's like kissing a gorilla's head.
(Monsters showed up on the torn screen
Of the Starlight Drive-In,
But he wasn't plagued by slippery doubt.)
He kissed the gorilla's head.
He then licked his lips and got to work,
The sourness like a handful of pennies.
I listened to Ricky for a while,
And then looked up to our professor,
His own face wild with gray hair and, I guess,
A lot of oral sex — scent that perked up
The ears of civil and uncivil dogs.
The prof said,
Freud puzzled over the meaning of dreams.
I wrote that down on a piece of paper,
And remembered last night's dream —
My right hand controlling the life
Of a plastic toy car. What did that mean?
I thought. I drew a face on this paper,
And then an ancient beard that was as old
As the road from
Damascus to a dirty drive-in in Fresno.
I touched my chin with its little bristle,
And I closed my eyes — Freud was in his tweed suit
And going down on a woman,
Her panties hooked around one ankle.
When he looked up,
Pennies were falling from his mouth
And his wife was clapping from the front seat
Of a triple feature.

MR. CINCO DE MAYO, THE WEIGHT LIFTER

He had high hopes for his ass
And great promise for his biceps
Hard as fists. Dinner plates in calves,
Rocks in stomach, slither of snakes
In his shoulders. I noticed his thighs
Were tan as holsters. What's it take?
I asked my cousin. He did a set of curls
And right there, under an effortless strain,
Veins flushed to the surface
Of arm and leg. Six years, he said.
Then in bikini briefs thin as kleenex,
He flexed. New veins surfaced,
Tumors of muscle, sweat, shine that was like Zen.
He turned, one delicate foot shot out,
And flexed again. More veins and muscle,
So much coming out
That I thought his spleen
Would suddenly appear like a fruit
To hang on his hip. He held his pose,
And I stepped back,
Fearing innards would splash out,
Flood the entire garage with stuff
I didn't want to see. Enough, I said,
And he turned again.
Right then he cried, Ouch!
His muscles collapsed like empires.
He lifted a foot and hobbled to a folding chair—
Sliver in a toe. Sweat flowed
And a line of skin on his stomach pouted.
But you're Mr. Cinco de Mayo!
I scolded, and my cousin shot up,
His chest quivering like a horse.
No ancient pierce could bring
Our local hero
Down.

THE SOPHISTS

How did one get by in 400 B.C.,
When the ox turned in a circle
And man whipped his slave
And the slave wondered
About the better jobs
Of his world. The sun made
Its point on the backs
Of oxen and slaves,
And the world flourished
Where holes were dug for
The dead. I hear the sophists
Talked for their living,
Perhaps under the grape arbor,
Or by a river, its surface
Pricked by starlight. The Western
Mind traveled east,
Just like the good jobs now,
But the sophists, those
Scattered few, remained
With their pencil shavings.
And what of Socrates with a beard,
That hive of lice and wisdom?
He drank himself dead on a stone
When what he needed was
A clubbing. Socrates,
The non-tenured fool,
Needed three days in a cave.
He needed a blind child
To stand on his shoulders
And steer him left,
No right, for the figs were
In season and her precious life,
A mighty hunger.

OUR FIVE SENSES

Aristotle threw his chops into a pomegranate
And proclaimed that we lived by senses.
He devoured bread, then a chicken,
His wallet-thick tongue dancing with pleasure.
He listened to the harmonica of his bad lungs.
He pulled in the smells of a salty sea.
He held up a feather
And said, "The eye beholds!"
He devoured an apple for more of the same
And concluded, "Taste and fiber!"
He made a good day of discovery
And then bedded down with a clean boy,
The bowl of his
Shiny bottom raised for the old master –
Four of five senses employed on a thrashing bed.

I pushed my arms into an ironed shirt,
Pulled together my five senses
And drove my date to the levee. I peeked
Out the window and, using my best line,
Said, "These stars died millions of years ago."
Her eyes lit up like a cat's
When a car passed, and then died.
I swallowed my fear
And threw my face like a hatchet
Into her neck, bruised
With hickies that weren't mine.
I employed two of my senses, taste and touch,
And then pulled away from her. I said,
"Aristotle liked boys but I like girls,
And did you know that smell is a good way
Of knowing a person?" A car passed.
Once again her eyes lit up,
Then went dead. She said, "Where do you learn
This stuff, Gary?" I swallowed again

And buried my face for more of the same.
I pulled away, tongue exhausted
From the thirteen laps around her neck.
I answered, "Junior college."
I rolled down the car window and sucked in
The spring air. Our city stunk.
We stood over the canal —
Tires floated
Along the reedy bank.
A five-eyed frog splashed
In the chemical runoff. Not far away,
Rednecks peed into the water,
Adding to its misery. We drove away
And parked under the whipping branches
Of a eucalyptus. I employed touch and taste
And shrugged my shoulders when my date
Called me by another dude's name. At seventeen,
I could only take so much of the world.
I guessed the frog with five eyes
Was living a nightmare. That evening,
I lived on my Aristotlian senses,
But closed my eyes
When I got to her neck, bruised with hickies,
Three of mine and others boiling up
Under a boy's sloppy hunger.

STARCHY CLOTHES

I put on pants and shirt, both ironed,
Both hard with milky starch,
And walked two miles to hear a string quartet.
I felt brand new in my starched clothes,
My legs stuffed in milk cartons,
My neck choked by a toilet roll.
I sat in the front row
And struggled to place a Life Saver on my tongue.
I looked around, my head turning awkwardly,
Stiffly. I recognized others
From Music Appreciation,
All of them with scrubbed faces
And straight as planks. They, too,
Had dropped their clothes into a galvanized bucket
And snowed the snowy starch on their clothes.
When the quartet appeared, also stiff,
I clapped like the Tin Man in the *Wizard of Oz*,
Just before he rusted, my hands coming
Together slowly – clap. . . . clap. . . . clap.
The quartet sawed their instruments back and forth,
Their tiny arms like the arms of praying mantises.
The music itself was slow,
But the evening was easy extra credit.
I sat tall as the letter A, tears in my eyes,
Then on my cheeks. My yawns could have pushed
The Nina, the Pinta, and the Santa Maria
Three times around the world. By the end,
My face was wet and I was out of breath.
I used both hands to stand up
And clap for the quartet.
On the way home, I prepared in my mind
The first line of my paper: "On a stiff evening
Of starched clothes, the audience
Cried with joy . . . no, joyfully cried . . .
no, cried oh, God, joyfully let this sucker end!"

I stepped one foot
Over the other, careful not to fall over.
I considered these options
With leftover tears in my eyes
And a wind filling my shirt
Like an almighty sail.

THE SCIENCE OF SOCKS

One sock was cotton,
The other a blend of nylon and cotton.
This much I knew. I sat on the edge of my bed
And held up these mismatched fish.
I wiggled into them anyway
And at school I walked around half-listening
To science, which was responsible for
The dye in these black socks.
And I half-listened in math,
Which was responsible for the numbers
Of these greedy stitches. I wrote in the margins
Of lined paper: our team is in last place.
At noon, I put on a hairnet and
Scooped chili beans onto plastic plates.
I could feel my feet. The left sock
Had slowed the blood in my foot,
And the right sock was hanging
Around my ankle, loose as an old inner tube.
I looked down at my work.
Science had piped fatness into these beans,
And math had counted out the tooth-marked silverware.
I itched beneath my hairnet
And itched in my feet. I searched
The cafeteria. I was catching on.
Physics, I thought, was the rise and fall of spoons
And the erratic splatter on white blouses.

GETTING AHEAD

A college job was pulling weeds
By the fistful – bitter tufts
Yanked with the chant,
She loves me, she loves me not.
I had this job in junior college,
And one Cinco de Mayo limped home
With a stone in my left shoe.
My brother had the better job
Of painting numbers on
Curbs. I clopped home,
Lame as a burro,
And floated in water,
Me a geography major
Without one turn in the Seven Seas.
I rolled in the bathtub
Like a whale and got out
Dripping. My hippie brother joked,
"O, geographer, where didst thee go?"
I answered, "O, Picasso
Of stencil-numbered curbs,
To the depths of our one-foot tub."
We ate Top Ramen
And looked from our balcony.
The whole town needed a weeding
And numbers on the curbs.
We were getting ahead. In economic
Geography, we took field trips,
Once to blink at blinking chickens
And another to a garment shop,
Mexican women like our mothers,
The voodoo of pins jutting from their mouths.
This didn't make me happy,
Nor did the trip
To a small airfield.
When the crop duster pilot cranked

The propeller, the wind of its blurring spin
Pulled homework from our arms —
Binder paper beating like gulls.
We screamed, laughed, and tiptoed for the homework,
For the Bs and As dancing above our heads —
That day, in propeller wind,
The true case of inflated grades.

RELIGIOUS CONVERSION

The elephant, eyes dripping,
Ate a bellyful of snails,
And long ago the hyena heard something funny,
Just after rock parted from water and became Africa.
I watched beasts rise from hiding,
Me the Christian teenager on a levee,
The sun another failure,
The wind a stink of recently slaughtered cattle.
I wanted my soul to be a boat loaded with animals,
Ostrich and penguin, rooster on the back of a buffalo,
All of us together. And why not toad and porcupine,
Alligator with its teeth
Like 32 staplers working at once?
Why not zebra and zebra's working brother, donkey,
And peacock with its tail like a fan of playing cards?
We could save ourselves. We needed an ark,
Even a log, to launch this salvation.
Like a reptile, I slid into the murky water
And paddled with hands, slowly at first,
Then with the fury of fins, gills, webbed feet,
The whip of tail and beat of wing,
All of us fleeing the perpetual slaughter,
The receding sun blood red at the edge of every town.

SCIENCE SAID

That The Beatles would make people nervous,
That kids would snap their fingers
Until they were exhausted
And unable to pull the trigger on a commie.
It was Sunday night, the enzymes
In our stomachs were slaughtering our chicken dinner.
I read the article, pushing peanuts into my mouth.
I looked up at my stepfather,
A large man in the recliner,
The hump-backed cigarettes stabbed in his ashtray.
Science said he was drunk. He stared at the television,
Where an hour earlier The Beatles had started
Singing Yeah-Yeah on Ed Sullivan
And he changed the channel
To *Gunsmoke,* where the town drunk was in jail
And repeating, If there is a will, there is a way.
I knew the truth in that saying,
And knew that if I snapped my fingers
To The Beatles I would exhaust myself
And become another person. I wanted badly
A music in my life, some Yeah-Yeah to cry in the shower.
I waited sixteen years for happiness.
I pushed peanuts into my mouth
And reread the article on science,
The prediction of muscle exhaustion
And our Asian enemy pinning our long, sissy locks
With one boot and kicking stars from our dreams
With the other. Today's youth, science said,
Was weak. Through the use of microscopes
Science eyeballed the swish of genes,
The subtle rhythm of Yeah-Yeah
In a mysterious chromosome.
Science added the strumming of guitars
Affected the young man's like or dislike for girls.

STATISTICS

Virginity is on the decline, the prof said,
And then handed out slips of paper.
His tongue was an arrow in his mouth,
And his meaty waist
Was the result of aimless eating.
I was thin as rope. I was nineteen,
And finally I got to vote on my failure.
In ignorant English I wrote, "I never got no sex,"
Then folded my slip of paper
And looked around, weasel-like,
Knowing that lots of the young women,
Most of the guys, were writing "Fuck yes,"
Some in old, block-headed English.
The prof walked up and down the aisle,
Collecting the slips,
His tongue now more like a spade,
His hands the spatulas of middle income.
He trembled when the votes were almost in.
Right there, in a three-unit class, on a table
Where other profs had rubbed their bottoms,
He counted out 27 fucks and 1 no fuck.
The students looked around the room like camels,
Some muttering. It was worse
Than I thought, no, better than I thought –
The class was one, red pulsating organ.
The prof asked, "What does this mean
In contemporary society?" Hands flew up
And the chatter began. I looked down
At my binder, already a failure in my first year
Of college, and sneezed. Spring blew
Through the window, blew the scent of cut grass,
Where bees played for their honey
Or were mowed without thought.

WINTER BREAK IN THE SNOW

Gray birds didn't help our hunger,
Those hoodlums of dead twigs
And frosted branches.
Or the walk up a slope where we unzipped
And wagged a long stream on a rock.
We knew no man or cow
Could stand knee-deep in this cold.

We returned to camp,
The wings of adventure matted to our shoulders.
We stared at the ghost of a smoldering fire
And rubbed our eyes. I told a story
About a forgetful man who ate his dog
And later was lonely
When he whistled
And pooch wouldn't come.
My friend almost laughed. We stirred the fire.
We needed coffee, but more than coffee
When I stood up and searched my pockets.
The car key was gone. We were eighty miles
From home, more lonely than the man
Who ate his dog.

The sun was high.
The bears of anger were wide awake.
When my friend shoved snow into my face,
We wrestled right over the tent
And sugar donuts. Ten minutes of this helped.
We sat quietly, listening to the grey birds
Shift on branches. We rose,
Drank water, and circled the dead fire,
Mourning our sorrow for a single key.
We burned the snow. We unzipped
In wind and searched the campsite
With lash after lash of a youthful hose.

EXTROVERT, INTROVERT, EXTROVERT

Shortly after the Ice Age,
Our prof said, we were extroverts.
It helped us keep warm,
All that action of yelling
And hitting each other really hard with clubs
And the like. We showed emotion in our faces —
Therefore the laughlines from the rhinoceros
Brought down with twelve spears and one mighty torch.
Therefore the pleats on our foreheads.
Therefore the shadowy creases around our eyes.
I wrote what my prof said. I was in junior college,
Not too bright, aware that I was an introvert.
A cloud roamed behind both of my eyes,
Obscuring the sight of the white panties
Inside my classmate's dress. I thought about them,
The panties. That was the part
Of me that was introvert,
The part that said I shouldn't stare outright
At this slippery kingdom. I took my notes,
A wiggle of lines.
More clouds roamed my eyes
Before the bell rang and I dragged my body
And leaned it against a faraway tree and screamed.
That part was left from my extrovert years
Out of the crib and into the highchair,
My shaker of a fist pounding
For milk and an animal cookie.
And now, at nineteen, I still screamed for milk,
A wet knuckle in my mouth.
This scream broke up all the clouds inside me.
I was a beast, an extrovert.
When I looked up, I felt my forehead was pleated
And my eyes narrow as flint.

Two young women came by, books in their arms
And ponytails fanning the fire.
I was the rhino sharpening his horn on the bark
Of an ancient tree.

POMPEII AND THE USES OF OUR IMAGINATION

Our history teacher, a southern fellow,
Said, "Close your eyes
And think back, back, back . . ."
This was a new way of sleeping
In an 8 o'clock class, the sun a pink scar
In our eastern window. He told us about Pompeii,
A bad-luck city, and how lava ran over the poor
And the rich alike. Since I was between
A "B" and an inflated "A," I did what I was told.
I closed my eyes and imagined a huge tamale
Run over by *mole* sauce, my only reference
To a smothered thing. On top of this tamale,
A chariot, crowned Gods, and an emperor in a robe.
There was a slave and slave's bloody ax.
Then there was a Nina, Pinta and Santa Maria,
O, my error, the wrong century.
I wiped out this image and returned to the flow
Of lava — jugs of wine, leather sandals, horses.
I saw a fountain, oxen, pigs and, for a second,
A covered wagon plugged with burning arrows.
My history was mixed up. I closed my eyes tighter,
And I returned to the lava flow —
Statues crumbling to their knees
And citizens caught in the hot river,
Their legs in the air.
I saw virgins run from the fire,
Soldiers in leather skirts and plumed helmets,
And then the covered wagon reappeared
With a sprout of more arrows.
My God, I scolded myself, What is wrong with you?
The history teacher repeated, "back, back, way back,"
I pulled together a harp, a bowl of grapes,
Figs like scrotums,
And then on the tamale I placed two cavemen,
No three, all with faces of actors —

Yul Brynner, Tony Curtis, and Kirk Douglas,
My heroes! They were going to fight the lava,
Push it back. But they slipped on the *mole* sauce
And slipped away on the lens of my tears.
I had gone too far. I was no good at history.
The covered wagon floated behind my closed eyes,
Then an astronaut, then George C. Scott.
I couldn't think right. A fork rose and fell
On that tamale, the steam uncurling,
Not unlike Pompeii when the land cooled,
Waves crashed, dogs sniffed the ruins,
And – my God, my error – the covered wagon with Moses
And Charleton Heston struggling for the reins!

MOVING OUR MISERY

If we peed into a canal,
If we added our youthful lash of salts to the water,
Misery would carry itself out of town.
I had been reading philosophy for World Religions
And concluded we were in big trouble.
Pericles was long dead, Socrates a rag in the earth,
And Galileo the lunar grit under a farmer's thumbnail.
One day, when a girl said, No, I love you as a friend,
I took my sorrow and cried into this canal,
My Buddha-shaped tears falling like an ancient rain.
The canal moved, just slightly, stirred the dead water.
I unzipped there and it flowed —
The junk on the bottom, the sofas and tires,
A wagon wheel, fishing tackle, a telephone booth,
A rubber glove pointing toward heaven.
The water flowed, and right there I needed my brother,
Three of his husky friends, maybe one dog,
A circus elephant. What was philosophy
But youthful water on an ancient current?
We could count one,
Two, three, then unleash ourselves
Into the canal
Until it flowed like the Nile,
Flowed through yellowish vapors.
Then it would snow,
Maybe rain, and the fish would return,
An egret or a smirking duck, all of nature at our feet,
Some of it climbing into our hair —
The cricket kick starting the night in our left ear.
We are, my friend, looking at the Garden of Eden,
Where Man walked nobly in front of the lion,
But jumped two steps
When the beast roared at his tasty bottom.

LOOK AROUND, PROF SAID

Keep your eyes open, Prof said,
And one night at Cuca's Restaurant
I was a spy—adultery in the third booth
Where a man and woman twirled spoons
And forks, the best they could do
On an evening as flat as water.
A brother tumbled into the cafe,
Dusted with dirt and bad luck,
Face creased with fissures
Ancient as the Nile. "I got onions!"
He said, "They just bagged,
Cue balls is what they be!"
Our brother eyed the cook,
Hat collapsed like a cake,
And he eyed Lupe the waitress,
The slaughter of enchiladas on her apron.
"Onions," he repeated. "It's good
In your kind of people's food."
The cook shook the cake on his head,
But in the third booth from the back,
The Julio Iglesias of oily evenings,
Held up two fingers, splayed like legs.

Our brother in this charade disappeared
He returned with two body bags
Of onions and strained as he dragged
Them up the aisle. So I took notes:
In Fresno, love is a man and a woman,
Each with a sack of onions,
Each with nothing but smeared plates.
I licked my pencil and wrote:
In adultery, tears can flood
When fingers peel the skin of onion,
Endless sheets with no heart in the center.

URBAN PLANNING

I wrote, "urban planning," on a computer card,
And when I turned to leave the counseling office
A student sobbed behind a closed door.
I listened, shamelessly,
And picked up, "he whipped my legs with a branch."
I left the office. Mid-March, and the
Weight of sun was no more than blossom on your shoulders.
(In July, it would be an anvil
And your anguish a black hole from your mouth.)
I walked around Fresno. After all,
I was an urban planner
And if I had my way, I would build a city
In which its citizens step over the stream
Every two or three blocks. The egrets smother
Their bills in the folds of feathers. Salamanders
And toads like a mess of knuckles
Flop among moss-colored stones.
Clouds pass with their hands open.
Rains fall with the coinage of October leaves.

I leapt as if I were stepping over a stream,
And leapt with a picture
Of this young woman with scarred legs.
The streams would bend, just out of view,
Then back into view, thin as the neck of a swan.
I was nineteen, so blameless
That the citizens could touch my arm for a blessing.
We needed water to rinse our tracks, that
And a fire in our leap and none on our legs.

The English prof told us to draw our ideas
And left the classroom feeling for the bottle
Of peach brandy inside his coat.
On binder paper,
I thought I could draw something bright
Between the lines. The idea
Was true as North and South,
East and West. So I drew smiling waves
Between the lines of binder paper
And as soon as the prof returned recapping his bottle
I planned to argue that rivers should be manageable.
So I drew this:

～～～

I added a Christian fish and Moses floating
In a basket. I looked around the room:
13 students clacked pencils between their top
And bottom teeth. 9 slept or snored with eyes open.
I looked at my binder paper.
I added more waves,
Fish and 22 Moseses in baskets, all asleep,
Like this class. The clock ate up
The hour and gave nothing back in return.
The prof never returned either.
I was the last to leave,
Right after a woman, her youthful bottom shimmying
Through the greasy door. And like a fish,
I wiggled upstream, the sunlight my water
And in the courtyard the other students
Igneous, hard-headed rocks.

COLLEGE POVERTY

I rationed my life,
Two crackers with their lucky shake of salt,
And chewed slowly. Across the table,
Beauty peeled back a burger —
Pickle and patty not round but square as a card.
I chewed and didn't mind. I memorized thirteen rivers,
Eight in Europe, five in North America.
I ate my crackers, then lay on the campus grass,
Hands behind my head. I studied the jittery leaves
Of an unlearned tree. I was a geographer,
The easiest of majors,
But hardest to put into action.
In my shoes, I couldn't get far.
In my bones, I would starve at the end of a road
Where the sun falls. No one is to blame for its collapse,
Or that Wednesday becomes Thursday before work was done.
I lay on the grass. I ate more crackers,
And watched clouds pull their tonnage of rain
And few flints of lightning. In time
We would arrive at the mathematics
Of geography. My lucky shake of salt would run out.
How young I was. I rolled like a cloud
Onto my belly. In the rooms inside my head,
I pictured professors with their dented globes.
I closed my eyes, then opened them —
A bee was weighing its honey with its frisky antennas,
Weighing and pulling the sweetness toward its thorax.
The bee blew away, not unlike those clouds,
And left me, cracker-thin, salty boy,
Hugging the perpetually hungry earth.

THE ESSAY EXAMINATION FOR WHAT YOU HAVE READ
IN THE COURSE WORLD RELIGIONS

From his cross Jesus said, Sit up straight,
And Buddha said, Go ahead and laugh, big boy,
And although no god, Gandhi said, Do onto others . . .
The last one didn't seem right. I relicked my pencil
And looked out the classroom window –
Two dudes smoking joints,
Yukking it up while I was taking a timed exam.
I noticed a stray dog, whose face was inside a paper bag.
This prompted me to look down at my feet –
My own lunch bag with three greasy splotches.
That was Pavlov, the reaction thing,
And at any moment I could start salivating.
I returned to my exam. I had to concentrate
And wrote, Zoroastrianism was a powerful religion
In a powerful time. Of Taoism, I wrote,
The split personality made you more friends.
I liked my progress. I looked out the window again –
The two hippie dudes now petting the dog
And blowing smoke into its furry face. I wrote:
Confucius was a good guy who stroked his whiskers.
I stalled here. The last part didn't seem right,
And it didn't seem right that our teacher
Should be reading the sports page while we suffered.
I got back to work. Who was Shiva?
When did Shinto start?
Why did the roofs of the pagodas
Swing upward? The rubbings
From my eraser snowed
To the floor and my tongue was black as plague.
The clock ate up the hour. The teacher put down
His newspaper and said, "You've been good students."

After class, I went around to see the hippie dudes,
Now passed out against the wall.

The dog lay between them, also snoozing,
The joint smoldering next to his furry face.
Unlike Ghandi, I thought, Let bygones
Be bygones, or something like that.
I opened my lunch bag with no judgment, no creed,
No French philosophical *nada*. I ate a hog
Of a burrito and then that ancient, mealy fruit,
The apple of our first sin.

LIVING BY THEORIES

A college friend said, "floating lint is a galaxy
Of our being," and I listened up,
A mug of hippie tea in one hand,
A stick of incense in the other.
When he said, "a spider crawls the length of solitude,"
I went to bed with my hair sweetened with smoke
And woke to a galaxy of lint
Floating in sunlight. I dressed,
Then went to my job of stenciling numbers
On curbs. In my town, people were easily lost,
And on amnesiatic nights, needed numbers to get home.
This was my theory — a whole town floating
Lost. Our citizens knitted sweaters
For their dogs and cats. I thought
About this while stenciling 1043 on a curb,
Within earshot of a judge sawing coffin-long boards
In his garage. The judge paid me.
I said, "You have a nice house, sir."
With this, his dog appeared in a knitted sweater,
The scent of talcum
In his fur. The dog looked me over, disgusted,
And turned with a wiggle — the pucker
Of its ass powdered
With talcum. I left with my stencils.
My theory was this: a giant onion was buried
Under our streets. Thus, we cried
Behind doors and beat each other fiercely.
The onion yellowed our lawns
And its fumes wavered from hot streets.
This was my theory as I painted 740 on the curb —
The lawn was yellow, almost dead.
I knew under its bed of roots lived an onion
That was skin and no heart.

I worked the tree-lined parts of Fresno.
The fumes dried the stenciled numbers,
And when the woman — a nurse
The height of coffin boards — paid me,
Her dog appeared, also dressed in a sweater.
His eyes weeped a black sludge,
For he had frolicked on the lawn
And was now paying the price. Afterwards
I walked a street where curb numbers were faded.
Business was poor. People were lost,
Their eyes wet and built up with sludge.
They were never going to get home.
I made my way through tears
And the watery vapors of streets.
When I opened the door, sunlight splayed
Through the room, all corners no more than lint
Floating by the fumes of a heartless onion.

BOOKS BY GARY SOTO

Junior College

Novio Boy

Buried Onions

New and Selected Poems

Jesse

Pieces of the Heart

Home Course in Religion

A Summer Life

Who Will Know Us?

Lesser Evils

California Childhood

Small Faces

Living Up the Street

Black Hair

Where Sparrows Work Hard

The Tale of Sunlight

The Elements of San Joaquin

PHOTO: CAROLYN SOTO

Gary Soto is a poet, playwright, essayist, and the author of several children's books. Widely anthologized, he is a frequent contributor to such literary magazines as *Harper's,* the *Ontario Review,* the *Iowa Review,* and *Poetry,* which has honored him with both the Bess Hokin and Levinson prizes. He has received the Andrew Carnegie medal, The Nation Discovery Prize, and an American Book Award from the Before Columbus Foundation, as well as fellowships from the Guggenheim Foundation, the National Endowment for the Arts, and the California Arts Council. A National Book Award Finalist for *New and Selected Poems* (Chronicle Books), Gary Soto divides his time between Berkeley and his hometown of Fresno, California.